This
Naure Storybook
belongs to:

_____

_____

SWEET CHESTNUT

BEECH

SYCAMORE

HAZEL

BIRCH

OAK

SCOTS PINE

For L.I.
C.B.

For Mrs Nock's class
C.V.

First published 2018 by Walker Books Ltd, 87 Vauxhall Walk, London SE11 5HJ

This edition published 2019

Text © 2018 Chris Butterworth Illustrations © 2018 Charlotte Voake

The right of Chris Butterworth and Charlotte Voake to be identified as author and illustrator respectively
of this work has been asserted by them in accordance with the Copyright, Designs and Patents Act 1988

This book has been typeset in Godlike and Charlotte Regular. Printed and bound in China. All rights reserved.

www.walker.co.uk 10 9 8 7 6 5 4 3 2 1

THE Things That I LOVE about TREES

Chris Butterworth

illustrated by Charlotte Voake

WALKER BOOKS
AND SUBSIDIARIES
LONDON • BOSTON • SYDNEY • AUCKLAND

It's spring!

And the thing
about trees that I love
in the spring is that
changes begin.

There are buds, like beads,
getting bigger
on the branches...

Trees are plants
(big ones!) and most plants
grow in spring.

6

21

9

The flower buds
on this plum tree
are opening into
blossom that's
buzzing with bees ...

8

Bees visit the blossom.
Pollen inside each
flower brushes
on to a bee,
who carries it
to the next flower.

and other buds
are opening into
brand new leaves.

The trees are
waking up!

New leaves are usually
a bright green colour
and still a bit
crumpled. They feel
soft to touch.

10

Birds and squirrels
build nests in the tree-tops,
safely hidden among
the new leaves.

In summer,
the thing about trees
that I love is how
big they look!

This one's as wide as our flats.

Trees do most of their growing in spring
and early summer. Their roots suck up water
from under the earth. In hot weather, a big tree
can drink as much as a bathful every day!

Summer trees are shady,
and so full of leaves,
when the wind blows they swish
like the sea.

Leaves use sunshine
to make food that
the tree
needs
so that it
can
grow.

By summer, leaves are
thicker, stronger and
darker-coloured than
they were in spring.

The blossom on the plum tree
has all dropped now,
but where each flower was
a little green plum
is growing.

A plum flower can't
make its fruit
without the pollen
that the
bees carried.

A new plum needs to swell
and ripen for several weeks
in the summer sun before
it's juicy and good to eat.

In autumn, the days are
shorter and cooler, so leaves start
to change colour and
begin to die.

The thing that I love
about trees in
the autumn is how
lots of them change colour:
from all shades of yellow,
to pumpkin orange
and fire-engine red.

As well as bright leaves,
I see tree seeds and ripe fruit:
nuts for the squirrels,
berries for the mice
and a sweet sticky plum
for a bird.

In the middle
of each plum is a seed
that can grow into
a new plum tree.

When the gales blow in,
the trees rain leaves!
(Catch one in the air,
and you can make
a wish.)

Some leaves that look
tiny high up on a tree,
turn out to be big
on the ground.

Not all trees lose their leaves
in autumn. The ones that do
are called "deciduous" trees.
Trees that keep their leaves
are called "evergreen".

23

In winter,
the thing that I love
about trees is how
bare they are.
You can lean
on the trunk
and look all
the way up to
the top.

(The tree's bark feels
hard and rough to touch.)

24

Trees that lose
their leaves
take a rest from
growing through
the dark,
chilly days
of winter.

Tree bark protects a tree from insects
and other animals who might eat it,
and also from too much heat or cold.

And when a storm comes,
thrashing the branches,
snapping off twigs
and rocking the trunk,
the tree's roots hold
it safe in the ground,

while it waits –

for the warm days of spring,
when the trees will begin
to wake up
all over again!

There are lots of games you can play and all kinds of things you can do with trees!

Build a den from big sticks and fallen branches.

Start a collection — pinecones, leaves, twigs, acorns, conkers.

Use a fallen tree as a giant climbing frame.

Make pictures and shapes with fallen leaves and sticks.

Hide away in an old hollow trunk or under low-hanging leaves.

Turn over old logs and bits of bark to go on a bug hunt. (A magnifying glass is handy.)

Stay very still and quiet to see
the wild creatures who make their
homes in the trees.

Index

Look up the pages
to find out all about
these tree things.
Don't forget to
look at both kinds
of words –

this kind

and

this kind.

A plum-tree note

There are lots of different varieties
of plum tree. They blossom and bear fruit
at different times, depending on what kind
they are and what climate they grow in.
The one in this book is based on the
European plum "Stanley".

SWEET CHESTNUT

BEECH

Note to Parents

Sharing books with children is one of the best ways to help them learn. And it's one of the best ways they learn to read, too.

Nature Storybooks are beautifully illustrated, award-winning information picture books whose focus on animals has a strong appeal for children. They can be read as stories, revisited and enjoyed again and again, inviting children to become excited about a subject, to think and discover, and to want to find out more.

Each book is an adventure into the real world that broadens children's experience and develops their curiosity and understanding – and that's the best kind of learning there is.

Note to Teachers

Nature Storybooks provide memorable reading experiences for children in Key Stages 1 and 2 (Years 1–4), and also offer many learning opportunities for exploring a topic through words and pictures.

By working with the stories, either individually or together, children can respond to the animal world through a variety of activities, including drawing and painting, role play, talking and writing.

The books provide a rich starting-point for further research and for developing children's knowledge of information genres.

Nature Storybooks support the literacy curriculum in a variety of ways, providing:
- a focus for a whole class topic
- high-quality texts for guided reading
- a resource for the class read-aloud programme
- information texts for the class and school library for developing children's individual reading interests

Find more information on how to use Nature Storybooks in the classroom at
www.walker.co.uk/naturestorybooks
Nature Storybooks support KS 1–2 English and KS 1–2 Science